# first
# animal
## encyclopedia
## seas and oceans

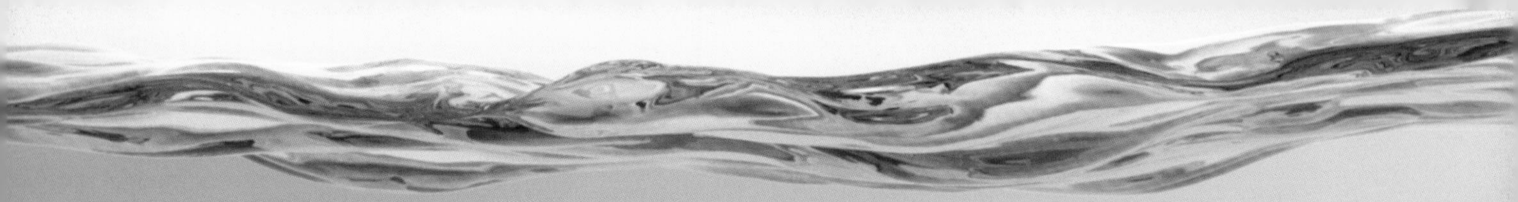

Published 2014 by
A & C Black
an imprint of Bloomsbury Publishing Plc
50 Bedford Square, London, WC1B 3DP
www.bloomsbury.com

ISBN HB: 978-1-4088-4305-5

Produced for Bloomsbury Publishing Plc by Dutch&Dane

The rights of Anna Claybourne to be identified as the author
of this work have been asserted by her in accordance with
the Copyrights, Designs and Patents Act 1988.

A CIP catalogue for this book is available from the British Library.

Picture acknowledgements:
Cover: All Shutterstock.
Insides: All Shutterstock, aside from the following images: p7 centre left
Solvin Zankl/Nature Picture Library; p19 top right Visuals Unlimited/
Nature Picture Library; p22 top right Alexis Rosenfeld/Science Photo
Library; p37 top left David Shale/Nature Picture Library; p39 bottom left
Solvin Zankl/Nature Picture Library; p51 centre left Doug Perrine/Nature
Picture Library; p53 centre left British Antarctic Survey/Science Photo
Library; p54 top right David Shale/Nature Picture Library; p55 top left
Solvin Zankl/Nature Picture Library; p56 top Dr. Ken Macdonald/Science
Photo Library; pp56-57 bottom Dr. Ken Macdonald/Science Photo Library;
p57 right P. Rona/OAR/National Undersea Research Program/
NOAA/Science Photo Library.

This book is produced using paper that is made from wood grown in
managed, sustainable forests. It is natural, renewable and recyclable.
The logging and manufacturing process conform to the environmental
regulations of the country of origin.

Printed about bound in China by C&C Offset Printing Co., Ltd

1 3 5 7 9 10 8 6 4 2

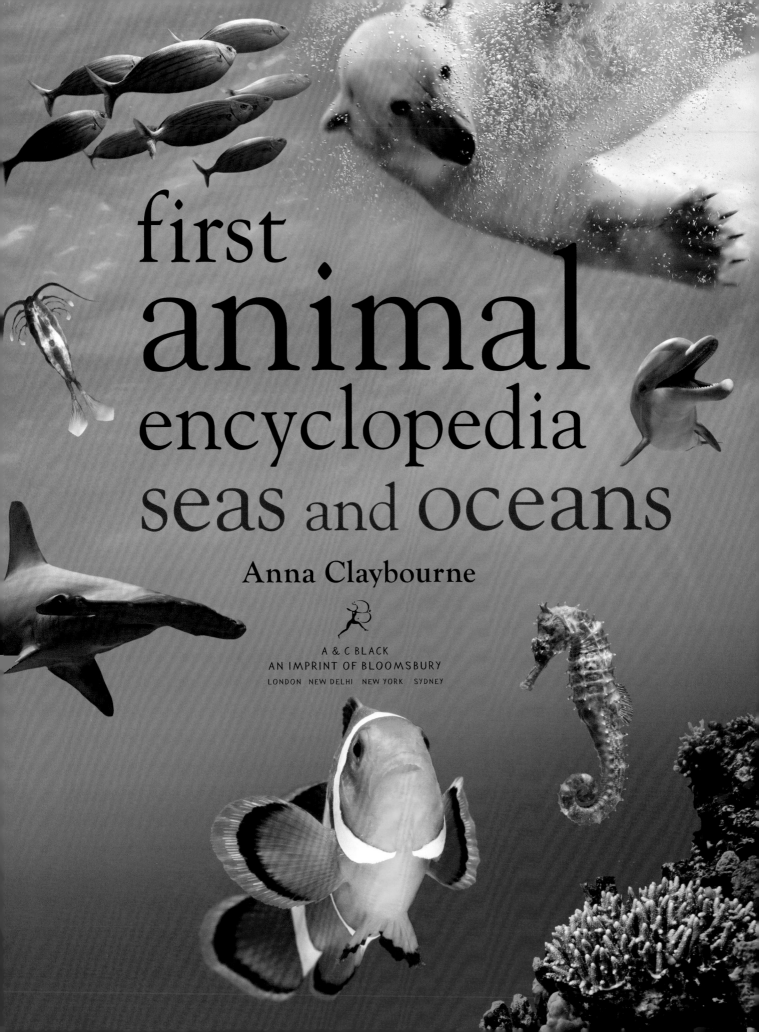

# first animal encyclopedia
## seas and oceans

### Anna Claybourne

A & C BLACK
AN IMPRINT OF BLOOMSBURY
LONDON  NEW DELHI  NEW YORK  SYDNEY

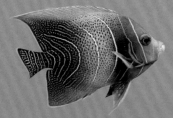

# Contents

# Ocean life

Oceans cover almost three-quarters of our planet. These watery worlds are filled with an amazing variety of living things. Many creatures are only found in the sea, such as octopuses, jellyfish and giant tube worms. There are also fish, shellfish, birds, mammals, sea snakes, seaweeds, and even ocean insects.

▲ The polar bear is the only ocean bear. It spends some of its time on land, but is also brilliant at swimming underwater.

## What is an ocean?

The word 'ocean' usually means a huge, salty sea covering a large area of the Earth. There are five main oceans. The biggest are the Pacific, Atlantic and Indian oceans. The Arctic and Antarctic (or Southern) oceans are at the top and bottom of the world.

▼ Jellyfish are strange-looking sea creatures. They are often partly see-through, with long, trailing tentacles.

# Seas and oceans

Seas are really no different from oceans – they are just smaller. The Red Sea, for example, is a narrow sea lying between Africa and Arabia. Seas can be part of larger oceans – such as the Caribbean Sea, which is in the Atlantic Ocean.

▲ The world's main seas and oceans are all joined together, as you can see on this map.

▼ Fierce, scary-looking viperfish are found in deep oceans.

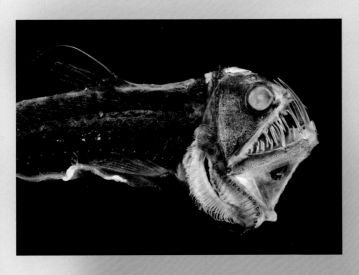

# Wide and deep

One reason there are so many sea creatures is that the oceans are truly huge. They are also very deep. Different types of creatures live at different levels, from the sunny shallows to the dark and gloomy depths.

◄ The Portuguese man-of-war is a bizarre, jellyfish-like animal. It uses its inflatable sail to float along on the sea's surface.

## AWESOME!

Oceans are so big and deep that there may be many sea creatures still waiting to be discovered. Scientists often find new ones, such as octopuses, sharks and strange, deep-sea fish.

# Fish in the sea

There are around 15,000 different species of ocean fish. They come in many different shapes and sizes. Some are as flat as a pancake, while others are long and skinny with no fins.

## What is a fish?

Fish are animals that breathe underwater using gills. They have a skeleton inside their bodies, and are cold-blooded. This means they stay a similar temperature to that of the water around them.

▼ Most fish have a smooth, streamlined body for slipping through water.

▲ You can see how the graceful seahorse got its name!

Tail

Head

Eye

Fin

Body covered in scales

Gills for breathing

Mouth

▲ Flying fish really do fly!

**AWESOME!**

Flying fish leap out of the sea, using their wing-like fins to glide along – as far as 200 metres in one go. They fly at speeds of up to 70 kilometres per hour.

## Sharks and rays

Sharks and rays are fish, too. Unlike most fish, they don't have scales – they have tough skin instead. Their skeletons are made of bendy cartilage, not bone. They eat fish, dolphins, seals, squid, shellfish, and plankton.

▲ Most fish lay eggs, but not all sharks do. Some, like the blue shark, give birth to live babies.

▼ Copperband butterflyfish use their long snout to feed on coral, shrimp and anemones.

## Fish food

Different types of fish eat different foods. Some are seaweed-nibblers, while others are fierce hunters. Some eat tiny ocean plants and animals called plankton. Some feed on coral, dead animals, and even on other fish.

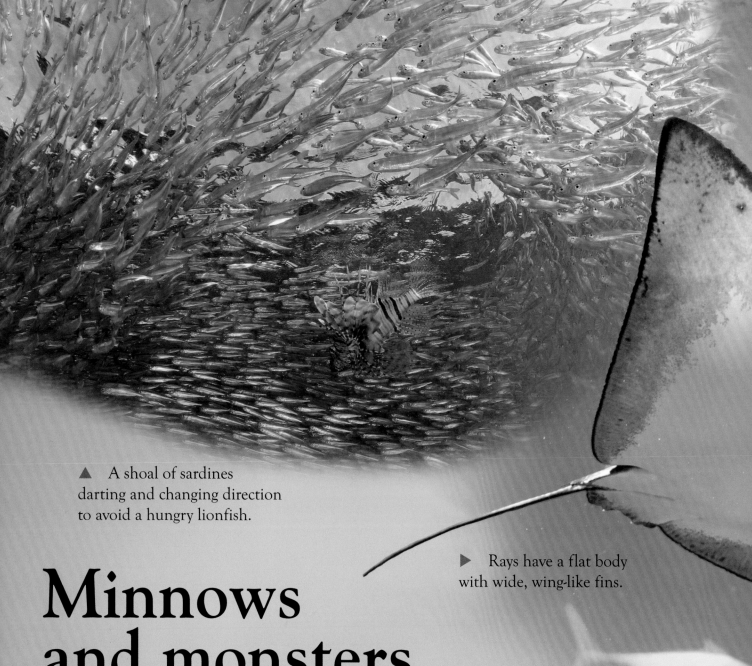

▲ A shoal of sardines darting and changing direction to avoid a hungry lionfish.

▶ Rays have a flat body with wide, wing-like fins.

# Minnows and monsters

Ocean fish range from tiny gobies, smaller than a grape, to enormous sharks as big as a bus. Some fish are so massive that they've been known to flatten whole boats when they leap out of the sea and crash back down.

## Swimming in shoals

Smaller fish often stick together in big groups, called shoals or schools. Sardines live in shoals of thousands or even millions of fish! Being in a group means fish can work together to watch out for danger.

## Filter feeders

Some of the biggest fish of all eat the smallest prey. The whale shark, the largest fish in the sea, moves along slowly, sucking in lots of water. Then it filters plankton and small fish from the water and swallows them.

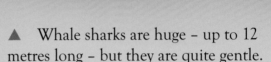

▲ Whale sharks are huge – up to 12 metres long – but they are quite gentle.

## Ocean giants

Besides enormous sharks and rays, two of the biggest fish in the oceans are the odd-looking sunfish and the giant oarfish.

▲ The ocean sunfish can grow to be three metres long and four metres from fin to fin, and can weigh more than a car.

▶ A sailfish can raise and lower the fin on its back, like a boat's sail.

## AWESOME!

Stout infantfish are the smallest fish – adult males are about seven millimetres long.

Sailfish are the fastest fish, reaching speeds of more than 100 kilometres per hour.

The deep-sea hagfish is the slimiest. It releases vast amounts of thick, snotty slime!

# Reptiles

Reptiles are scaly-skinned animals. They include snakes, lizards, crocodiles and others. Most live on land, but some are sea creatures. Reptiles are cold-blooded, which means they can't warm up their own bodies. They like to live in warm, tropical waters.

## Sea snakes

Sea snakes glide through the ocean using their paddle-like tails. Like other sea reptiles, they swim near the ocean surface, so they can come up for air when they need to. Some sea snakes have a deadly, poisonous bite.

▼ Sea snakes are often stripy, like these two banded sea kraits.

# Turtles

Sea turtles have a shell on their back, and flippers for swimming. Some are huge – the leatherback turtle's shell can be up to two metres long! Turtles mostly live in the sea, but lay their eggs on the shore.

◄ After mating, the female crawls up onto a sandy beach. She uses her back flippers to dig a nest in the sand.

▲ Green sea turtles swim long distances to their breeding areas to find a mate.

► She lays more than 100 eggs in the hole and covers them over with sand.

▲ After 50–60 days, the baby turtles hatch, dig themselves out, and crawl down to the sea.

# Ocean-going crocs

American and saltwater crocodiles can live in the sea, as well as in rivers and swamps. The saltwater croc can grow to seven metres long. It's the world's biggest reptile.

## AWESOME!

There is just one sea lizard – the marine iguana. It lies on rocky beaches to warm up in the sun, then dives into the sea to nibble on seaweed.

# Ocean mammals

Most mammals live on land, but a few have adapted to life in the ocean. They still need to breathe air, but some can hold their breath for up to an hour to go on deep ocean dives.

## Whales and dolphins

Whales and dolphins have smooth skin and streamlined, fish-shaped bodies. Instead of nostrils, they have a blowhole on top of their head, to make it easier to breathe while swimming.

▼ How can you tell a dolphin from a shark?

**Dolphin features**

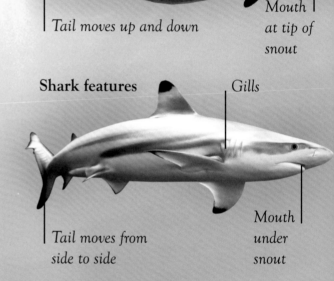

No gills

Tail moves up and down

Mouth at tip of snout

**Shark features**

Gills

Tail moves from side to side

Mouth under snout

◄ Seals are fast and nimble in the water – but on land, they have to flop and wriggle around.

## The seal family

Seals, sea lions and walruses are furry sea mammals. They are all hunters, feeding on fish, shellfish, crabs, seabirds or squid. A thick layer of fatty blubber, under their skin, helps to keep them warm.

# Polar bears

Polar bears have thick, white fur
to blend in with ice and snow,
and big front paws for swimming.
Polar bears swim long distances
to find seals to hunt for food.

▲ Polar bear cubs have a close bond with their mother. They feed on her nutritious milk.

## The strange sirenians

Manatees and dugongs are large,
slow-moving sea mammals that
live in warm, shallow seas. They
like to wander around, snooze
and graze on seagrasses, which
grow on the shallow seabed.

◀ Dugongs and manatees are often called sea cows – because of the way they hoover up seagrass.

▶ When an orca jumps,
its whole body comes out
of the water – and then
smashes down again.

## AWESOME!

Scientists have found
that some sea mammals
are very clever. For example,
orcas (killer whales) make
waves to wash seals off the
ice so they can catch them.

# Birds of the sea

On a trip to the seaside, you might hear the squawks and cries of the seagulls, terns, puffins or penguins that live there. Seabirds often nest in huge groups, called colonies, on sea ice or cliffs, and hunt for food in the ocean.

▲ The wandering albatross is the biggest species, with a wingspan of three to four metres.

## Penguins

Penguins can't fly, as they have flippers instead of wings. They use them for swerving and steering underwater, to chase fish and avoid hunters such as leopard seals. Penguins live in the southern hemisphere of the world, including the freezing-cold continent of Antarctica.

## The soaring albatross

Albatrosses are enormous, swooping seabirds that glide huge distances across the ocean. They can spend up to ten years out at sea, only returning to land when they are ready to nest and have chicks.

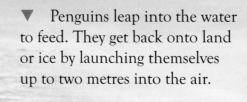

▼ Penguins leap into the water to feed. They get back onto land or ice by launching themselves up to two metres into the air.

Gannets (below) catch fish by folding up their wings – to form a rocket shape – and plunging into the sea at speeds of up to 120 kilometres per hour.

# Nesting in numbers

Seagulls and their relatives – skuas, petrels, puffins and gannets – are the most common seabirds. Their huge nesting colonies can completely cover a craggy cliff or island, turning it white with seabirds and droppings.

▼  This is a puffin nesting colony on Farne Island, off the northeast coast of England, UK.

◄  Adult puffins take it in turns to keep their eggs warm and to feed their young.

17

# Molluscs

The mollusc family includes snails, shellfish, octopuses and squid. There are more mollusc species than fish species in the sea, and they make up a quarter of all types of sea creatures.

## Seashells

The creatures that live in seashells are mainly molluscs. If a shell has two matching parts, held together with a hinge, it's a bivalve mollusc – such as an oyster, mussel or scallop. Bivalves feed on tiny bits of food in the water. Some anchor themselves to rocks, while others, such as scallops, can swim by flapping their shells.

▼ Giant clams can grow to more than a metre across.

▼ Nudibranchs have stinging cells, similar to those of jellyfish.

## Sea snails

A spiral-shaped or cone-shaped shell probably belongs to a sea snail. Sea snails usually have thicker, stronger shells than land snails, helping to protect them from predators such as crabs. Many use a sharp tongue to scrape algae off rocks.

## Sea slugs

Sea slugs are like land slugs – they are related to snails, but don't have shells and so need other ways to protect themselves. They often have bright, vivid colours and patterns to warn hunters that they are poisonous or taste revolting. Some can squirt acid and others have a venomous sting.

▶ Sea snails eat soft foods such as marine plants and algae.

# Octopuses and squid

The mollusc family also includes cephalopods, such as octopuses, cuttlefish and squid. The name cephalopod means 'head-foot', as their many legs (actually called arms) are attached to their heads.

## Amazing octopuses

Octopuses have an astonishing ability to change not just their colour, but their shape and texture, too. In seconds, a common octopus (right) can switch from smooth and white to looking like a bunch of brown, speckled, frilly seaweed.

Eye

Head

Mantle – the main body area

Arms with suckers for holding prey

A 'siphon' squirts water to push the creature along.

▲ Parts of a common octopus.

◀ A blue-ringed octopus can blend in with its surroundings, then suddenly flash its bright, electric blue ring markings.

# Cuttlefish

Cuttlefish are not fish, but molluscs with eight short arms and two longer tentacles. They can send signals to each other by flashing quick-changing colours and patterns across their skin.

## AWESOME!

The nautilus (above) is the only type of modern cephalopod that has a shell. But in prehistoric times there were huge, octopus-like creatures with shells, called ammonites (below).

▲ Cephalopods, such as this cuttlefish, are relatives of slugs and snails. They do not have any bones.

# Squid

Squid come in a huge range of sizes. The smallest is the pygmy squid – it's no bigger than your little finger! The biggest squid, the giant and colossal squid, can reach around 14 metres long.

▶ These Caribbean coral reef squid are looking for prawns, crustaceans and fish to feed on.

# Crustaceans

Crustaceans, such as crabs, lobsters and prawns, are very common. They get their name from their 'crust' – their hard shell. They are related to insects and spiders. Like them, they have an 'exoskeleton' – a skeleton on the outside of the body.

▲ People sometimes catch and eat isopods.

## Crabs, lobsters and prawns

These crustaceans all have ten legs. The front legs often have large claws or pincers for holding on to food. Most of these animals are scavengers, meaning they eat whatever they can find.

## Giant isopod

This many-legged, creepy-crawly crustacean looks a bit like a pale pink woodlouse. It is related to the woodlouse, but it is much bigger – up to 40 centimetres long – and it lives on the deep seabed.

▼ A Caribbean spiny lobster.

*Two antennae (for sensing)*

*Exoskeleton (hard shell)*

*10 legs*

Head

Claws

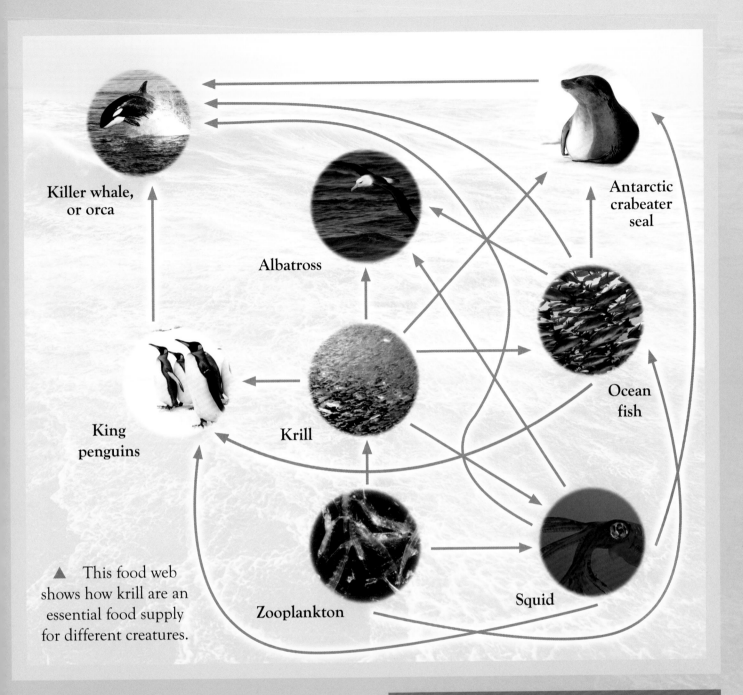

Killer whale, or orca

Albatross

King penguins

Krill

Zooplankton

Squid

Ocean fish

Antarctic crabeater seal

▲ This food web shows how krill are an essential food supply for different creatures.

# Krillions!

Krill are small, pinkish crustaceans, similar to shrimp. There are trillions of them – so many that, if all of them were put together, they would weigh more than all the humans on Earth! They are very important, because many other sea creatures rely on them for food.

## AWESOME!

The tiny snapping shrimp, just four centimetres long, makes one of the loudest sounds in the sea. When it snaps its claw shut, it creates a super-powerful sound wave, strong enough to break glass.

◀ Crown-of-thorns starfish usually have around 20 arms.

# Starfish and sea urchins

Starfish and sea urchins belong to a bizarre family of sea creatures called echinoderms. Their name means 'spiny skin' and they all have spines, prickles or bumps.

## Many-pointed stars

Most starfish have five arms, though they can have more. Starfish are hunters, and eat shellfish, crabs and sea worms. There are around 1,500 different species of starfish, and some can have as many as 40 arms!

# Hunting and feeding

A starfish eats its prey by holding it tight, then pushing its stomach out of its mouth and into its prey. The stomach digests the meal and turns it to liquid, which the starfish can then suck back into its body.

▲ Starfish move about using rows and rows of tiny, tube-like feet.

## Sea cucumbers

Like other echinoderms, the soft, sausage-shaped sea cucumber has five sections. The mouth is at one end, and five rows of tiny feet run along the body. Sea cucumbers eat bits of old food and other animals' poo.

## AWESOME!

If a starfish loses an arm, it can grow a new one to replace it. Not only that – the cut-off arm can sometimes grow into a whole new starfish!

▼ The skin of a sea cucumber feels a bit like leather.

## Sea urchins

Sea urchins are round or oval, with a hard, spiny shell made up of ten sections. The urchin sticks its mouth out of a hole at the bottom to feed on algae.

▼ These Diadema sea urchins have very long, dark spines.

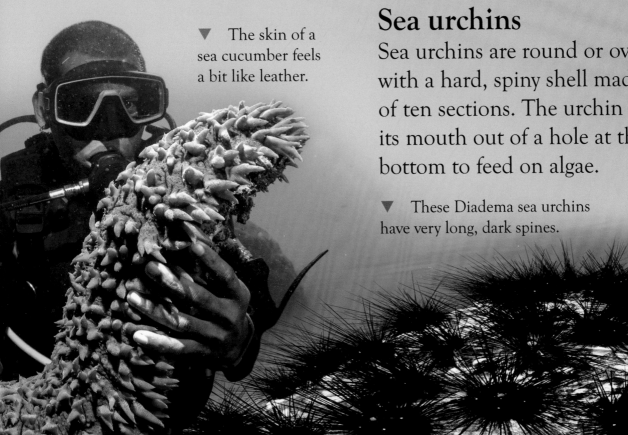

# Jellyfish and sea anemones

Jellyfish, or jellies, are very strange animals. They have no brains, though some do have nerves that can detect movement and light. Some jellies are deadly.

## Jellyfish parts

A jellyfish has a rounded body at the top, called a bell, with dangling tentacles underneath. Its mouth is in the middle, with arm-like parts around it. Some jellies drift around, while others can swim along by squeezing their bell to squirt water out.

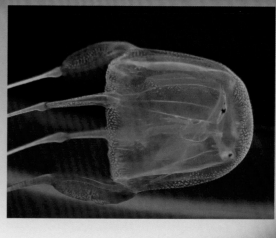

▲ The box jellyfish is almost see-through. It has a seriously deadly sting.

## AWESOME!

The terrifying-looking lion's mane jellyfish is the biggest jelly in the oceans. Its bell grows to two metres across, and its tentacles can be 60 metres long!

▼ Jellyfish catch prey in their stinging tentacles.

## Sailing ship jelly

The Portuguese man-of-war gets its name from a type of sailing ship. It has a gas-filled 'sail' that floats on the ocean surface, stopping it from sinking. It isn't a 'true' jellyfish, but it does have stinging tentacles for catching prey.

▲ Sometimes, man-of-war jellies drift together in the wind and get washed ashore.

## Sea anemones

Sea anemones are related to jellyfish, but they stay stuck to rocks or coral. They reach out to grab food such as small fish and sea worms. Like jellyfish, they have tentacles that can stick to and sting their prey.

▶ Sea anemones are named after the anemone, a flower found on land.

27

# The Pacific Ocean

The Pacific is the biggest of all the world's oceans, covering a third of the globe. The word *pacific* means 'peaceful' – but as well as calm waters, this ocean has plenty of storms.

## Floating feast

The Pacific contains a LOT of plankton – tiny plants and animals drifting in the water. Plant plankton float near the surface and use energy from sunlight to grow. Animal plankton often feed on plant plankton. Together, they provide food for larger sea creatures.

▲ The Pacific Ocean has many small islands and coral reefs, as well as vast areas of open water.

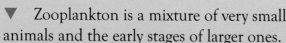
▼ Zooplankton is a mixture of very small animals and the early stages of larger ones.

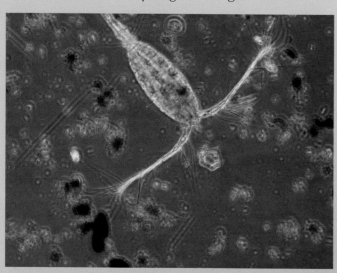

◀ A loggerhead turtle can travel at 24 kilometres per hour.

▶ Humboldt penguins breed on the coasts of Peru and Chile, in South America.

# Currents of life

Currents are streams of fast-flowing water in the sea. Animals such as whales, saltwater crocodiles and loggerhead turtles use the Pacific currents to swim long distances.

# Cold current

As the Humboldt Current flows past South America, it sucks deep water up to the surface. This water is filled with chemicals from the seabed that provide food for plankton. Fish flock to feed on the plankton, followed by seals and seabirds.

# Humpbacks of Hawaii

Huge humpback whales visit the cooler areas around the poles to feed on plankton, krill and small fish. They then swim to the warm, tropical seas around Hawaii, Mexico or the Philippines to mate.

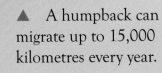 ▲ A humpback can migrate up to 15,000 kilometres every year.

## AWESOME!

The Pacific Ocean contains the Mariana Trench, the deepest point in all the world's oceans. The bottom of the trench is almost 11 kilometres deep!

29

# Along the coast

A coastline is a strip of land next to the sea. The world has more than 350,000 kilometres of coastline – that's almost as long as the distance to the Moon!

▼ A walrus rookery, where the adults raise and protect their offspring.

## Coastal nurseries

For many animals, the seashore is a safe place to lay eggs. Turtles hide their eggs under the sand, while seabirds such as guillemots nest on cliffs, where it's hard for hunters to reach their eggs. Seals and walruses use the coast for their nurseries, known as rookeries, where the babies are safer from predators.

# Dune dwellers

The wind blows sand into heaps, or sand dunes, which are often covered in tough seashore grasses. Animals such as lizards, snakes and burrowing mice live among the dunes, feeding on insects or plants.

▲ Natterjack toads can lay their eggs in the warm, freshwater pools found on coastal sand dunes.

## AWESOME!

Fulmar chicks keep themselves safe, while their parents are fishing for food, by squirting predators with a jet of stinky, fishy vomit!

# Seashore feeders

Animals visit the seashore when the tide goes out to feed on coastal sea creatures such as shellfish, sea worms and crabs. Oystercatchers, for example, have specially adapted beaks for prising open shellfish or digging deep in the sand for worms.

▶ The tip of this oystercatcher's bill is pointed – perfect for picking up worms.

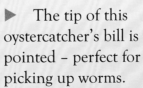

# High and dry

At the coast, the sea moves up and down the beach twice a day, due to the tides. At high tide, the beach is covered in seawater. At low tide, it's left empty. So, the animals that live here have to survive in two very different habitats.

▼ Mussels open their shells underwater to feed, but clamp them tightly shut to stay safe and damp at low tide.

▲ Mussels, starfish, crabs and sea anemones are among the creatures found in tide pools.

## Open and shut
Molluscs with shells are often found on beaches. Bivalves such as oysters and mussels clamp the two halves of their shells tightly together. Sea snails and limpets clamp the openings of their shells firmly onto a rock, and stay there until the water comes back.

# Rock pools

On rocky beaches, seawater can get caught in cracks and hollows in the rocks as the tide goes out. This forms rock pools, or tide pools, where sea creatures can shelter at low tide.

## AWESOME!

If you see a coil of sandy sediment on the surface of a beach, you've probably discovered a lugworm burrow. As the worm digs down, it passes sediment through its body and then ejects it to the surface. This is called a worm cast.

# Under the beach

Even when the surface of a beach is dry, it's damp underneath. Seashore crabs and worms can hide under stones or in burrows in the sand. This helps them to escape predators and also stops them from drying out in the sun.

▼ Ghost crabs get their name from their ability to blend into the background and 'disappear'.

◄ Crab-eating macaques are found in Southeast Asia.

# Mangrove forests

Mangrove trees grow on seashores in tropical regions, and they can survive being in salty water at high tide. Their roots stick up out of the sand or mud. The trees and their roots are home to lots of animals.

## A place to hide

Mangrove roots stick out of the sand and act like a cage. Fish, shellfish, crabs and turtles can hide there from hunters, such as sharks, while other sea creatures use the roots as a safe place to lay their eggs.

## Swimming cats

In the massive Sundarbans mangrove forest, in India and Bangladesh, fishing cats swim after fish and crabs, and can even dive underwater to catch their meals.

◄ Not many cats like getting wet, but fishing cats are at home in the water.

▲ Male proboscis monkeys make a funny *kee-honk* sound through their long noses.

# Mangrove monkeys

The crab-eating macaque feeds on fruit and crabs on beaches and mudflats. The funny-looking proboscis monkey swims around salty mangrove swamps in search of its favourite fruits.

# Walking fish

Mudskippers feed on worms, insects and shrimp that live in the mud around mangrove roots. To reach them, these strange fish can crawl out of the sea and hop along on the mud, using their front fins like a pair of legs.

▶ Mudskippers keep a frothy mixture of air and water in their gills, when out of water, so that they can breathe.

## AWESOME!

Bengal tigers in the Sundarbans National Park – in West Bengal, India (Asia) – often go for a swim in the many mangrove forests found there.

3

# The Atlantic Ocean

The Atlantic is the world's second largest ocean. An undersea mountain range, called the Mid-Atlantic Ridge, runs all the way down its middle.

▶ The Atlantic Ocean includes many smaller seas and bays.

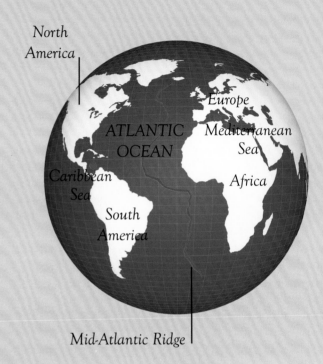

North America

Europe

ATLANTIC OCEAN

Mediterranean Sea

Caribbean Sea

Africa

South America

Mid-Atlantic Ridge

## Dolphins on display

There are more than 30 species of dolphin. They often surf along the waves made by boats and ships, an activity called 'bow riding'. They can also leap right out of the sea, twisting, spinning or flipping over in amazing acrobatic displays.

▶ Bottlenose dolphins can reach speeds of over 30 kilometres per hour.

◀ The Dumbo octopus floats just above the seabed to look out for prey.

Atlantic salmon start their life in rivers, then swim out into the Atlantic Ocean to feed and grow. When they are ready to mate and lay eggs, they swim all the way back to the stream where they were born!

## Life on the ridge

Most of the Mid-Atlantic Ridge lies far below the ocean surface, at a depth of about 3,000 metres. Dumbo octopuses have been found there. They're named after their fins, which look like the ears of a cartoon elephant.

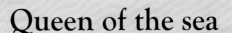

## Queen of the sea

The Atlantic Ocean includes the warm, tropical Caribbean Sea. Here, there are lots of islands surrounded by shallow waters and coral reefs. Many beautiful seashells are found here, such as that of the queen conch, a very large sea snail.

▶ The queen conch's white and pink shell can grow to 30 centimetres long. People in the Caribbean often eat the giant snail inside.

# The open ocean

The wide, deep part of the ocean lies far away from land. It is also known as the 'pelagic zone'. There is plenty of space here, so it's a good home for large, fast creatures as well as much smaller animals.

## Pelagic birds

Sooty terns and albatrosses can spend years out at sea, landing on the surface to catch fish. Macaroni penguins spend most of the year in the open sea, feeding on fish and krill, only coming ashore to breed.

▶ Macaroni penguins sometimes swim more than 10,000 kilometres in search of food.

▼ Sardines swimming in the bright, sunlit zone.

## Up and down

Scientists divide the open ocean into layers, or zones, from top to bottom.

## The sunlit zone (0–200 metres deep)

Sunlight shines into the water here, so that plant plankton and seaweed can grow as food for ocean animals. The water contains lots of oxygen for the animals to breathe.

# The twilight zone
## (200–1,000 metres deep)
There is very little light here, and the water is colder, so there are fewer animals.

▲ A sperm whale can hold its breath for more than an hour and dive down to over 2,000 metres.

# Midnight zone
## (Below 1,000 metres deep)
Deep down in the open ocean it is completely dark. The creatures that live here often have bodies that they can 'light up' naturally.

## AWESOME!

There are very few large hunters on the deep-sea floor. This bluntnose six-gill shark is one of them. It scavenges for left-overs on the seabed by day, and creeps up to feed on living prey at night.

▼ Lanternfish are named after the bright spots of light on their body.

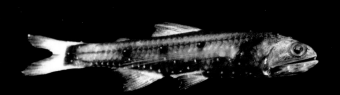

# Ocean hunters

In the open ocean, it can be very hard to hide. There are predators everywhere, attacking from all directions.

## Feeding on fish

The main food on the open ocean menu is fish. Shoals of sardines, capelin, anchovies and other small fish are devoured by bigger fish, sharks, penguins, squid, whales and dolphins.

▼ These lemon sharks have pale skin, which hides them against the sandy seabed as they hunt.

▼ The blue-spotted stingray has bright patterns on its skin to warn predators to stay away. It has two venomous spines in its tail.

## Hunting with venom

Venomous animals inject killer chemicals into their prey, using fangs, spines or tentacles. Jellyfish use stinging tentacles to hunt. This means they can catch other animals even though they are neither strong nor fast.

▲ A whale shark filters about 6,000 litres of water every hour, taking small shrimp and plankton from the water.

## Filter feeders

Some larger sea creatures move slowly, and have to catch fish a different way. Whale sharks suck in vast amounts of seawater, along with the plankton and fish it contains. Their huge mouth lets the water flow back out again, but keeps the food trapped inside.

# On the move

In the open ocean, many sea creatures have to move fast to get away from danger, or to catch prey. Others must swim long distances to feed or breed.

▲ These sea lions are using their flippers to change direction quickly.

## Top speed

Some animals have adapted to move easily through water. Creatures such as dolphins have a long, pointed shape that helps water to flow past them. Their power comes from flexing their strong, muscular tail.

▼ The blue marlin is one of the fastest fish in the sea, travelling almost 100 kilometres per hour.

## Flippers

The wings, fins or legs of some animals have adapted to become flat, paddle-shaped limbs that are perfect for swimming. Flippers are also very useful for steering.

# Unusual movers

Octopuses and squid have a siphon, which is a funnel sticking out of their bodies. They can fill themselves up with water, then squirt it out of the siphon. This pushes them forward.

To escape danger, flying fish paddle incredibly fast with their tails to launch themselves out of the sea. Then they angle their wing-like fins so that they can glide like a bird.

## AWESOME!

Huge sharks, whales and rays launch themselves out of the water, then fall back down with a huge splash. This is known as breaching.

# The Indian Ocean

The third largest ocean in the world is the Indian Ocean. It lies between Africa and Asia, and surrounds most of India. It is mainly a warm, tropical ocean with lots of coral reefs.

## Warm waters

Warmer, tropical seas hold less oxygen gas. This means that the Indian Ocean cannot support as much plankton, krill and fish as other oceans. However, many sea mammals and reptiles prefer the warm water, so there is plenty of life here.

▲ The Indian Ocean has many islands, including Madagascar and Sri Lanka.

◀ The lionfish is a venomous species found in warm, tropical waters.

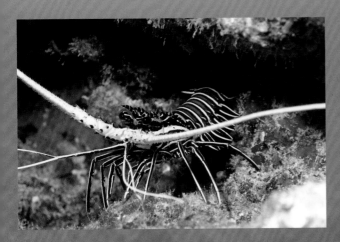

▲ This clever mimic octopus, found in the Indian Ocean, can copy the appearance of other sea animals, often to avoid being eaten.

## Shallow reefs

Many types of coral grow best in warm water, and the Indian Ocean has some incredible coral reefs. They grow near beaches and around islands. The ocean's reef creatures include the venomous lionfish, the well-hidden spiny devilfish and the cunning mimic octopus.

▼ The poisonous spiny devilfish, or demon stinger, partially buries itself in the seabed during the day.

▲ Spiny lobsters inhabit tropical reefs all over the Indian and Pacific oceans.

# Coral reefs

Reefs lie under the surface of the sea, making an area of shallow water. Reefs can be made of rock, sand or coral, which is a kind of seashell made by tiny sea creatures called coral polyps. Coral reefs grow slowly, but can cover huge areas over time.

## How coral grows

The polyps in a colony are linked together by tiny tubes, so that they can share food. Each polyp builds a hard shell around its base. As new polyps are born, they grow on top of the old ones. This is how the hard coral grows bigger and bigger.

▲ A coral polyp opening up to feed.

◄ Many different species of coral polyp can be found on one coral reef.

# Coral reef dwellers

Coral reefs are full of life. The coral provides nooks and crannies where fish, shrimp and molluscs can avoid enemies and lay their eggs. Reefs are also a place to eat. Seaweed grows on and around the coral, providing food for turtles, sea urchins and crabs.

▲ Most octopuses are nocturnal, but the cyanea octopus comes out during the day.

## AWESOME!

The Great Barrier Reef is a huge string of coral reefs and coral islands, about 2,500 kilometres long. It is the largest structure ever built by living things!

Great Barrier Reef

AUSTRALIA

# By day and by night

Coral reefs form in shallow seas in warm places. During the day, the water is lit up by sunshine – and diurnal (daytime) animals are active. At night, these animals find places to hide or rest. Then the nocturnal reef-dwellers come out to feed.

▼ Hawksbill turtles are active during the day.

▲ This harlequin shrimp is a night feeder. Here, it flips a starfish over to feed on the soft tube feet and tissues underneath.

47

# Living together

The different creatures on a coral reef live together in a way that helps them all survive. This is called an ecosystem. Other habitats, such as an icy sea or a mangrove forest, have their own ecosystems, too.

▼ The food web below is an example of a coral reef ecosystem. The arrows show the direction of the food energy as the animals eat other living things.

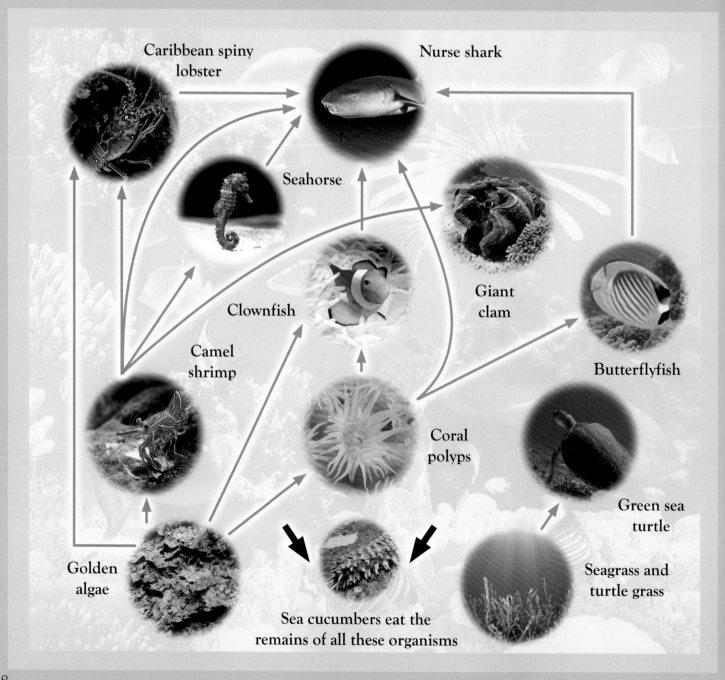

Caribbean spiny lobster

Nurse shark

Seahorse

Clownfish

Giant clam

Butterflyfish

Camel shrimp

Coral polyps

Green sea turtle

Golden algae

Sea cucumbers eat the remains of all these organisms

Seagrass and turtle grass

## How does it work?

Because coral provides food and shelter, it attracts other creatures, such as small fish and shellfish. They attract hunting animals that want to feed on them, such as octopuses. Bigger hunters such as sharks then come to feed on them, too. The ecosystem ends up with a mixture of different creatures that rely on each other for food.

Coral reefs only cover 0.2 per cent (or one 500th) of the seabed. Yet around a quarter of all species of sea creatures live on or around them!

▲ A grouper lets a cleaner shrimp pick lice from its body and old food from between its teeth.

## Scavengers

Who eats the animals at the top of the food web? When animals die, their bodies start to decay. Their remains get eaten by scavengers, animals such as crabs and sea cucumbers. In this way, the cycle goes around and around.

▼ A sea cucumber crawls across a reef, taking in bits of old coral so that it can extract tiny, living creatures from it as food.

## Helping each other

Two species sometimes live together to help look after each other. This is called symbiosis. For example, large fish called groupers visit areas where tiny cleaner shrimp live. The fish gets cleaned, while the shrimp gets a meal!

# The Arctic Ocean

The Arctic Ocean lies around the North Pole, the most northerly part of the Earth, and it's very cold. In winter, the ocean freezes. In summer, some parts of it melt.

▲ The Arctic Ocean is surrounded by Alaska (USA), Canada, Iceland, Russia and northern Norway.

## Cold water life

The Arctic Ocean is icy cold, but it has a lot of plant plankton in it, especially in the summer. This provides food for other creatures. There are many fish, molluscs, dolphins and whales. Humpback whales visit the ocean to feed.

◄ Beautiful, pale-skinned beluga whales live in the Arctic Ocean's coastal waters. They feed on fish and crustaceans.

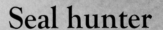

▶ A hungry polar bear is looking for seals swimming below the ice.

## AWESOME!

The Greenland shark, one of the biggest sharks in the world, can grow to seven metres long and lives in the Arctic. It prefers deep, cold waters – but it sometimes visits shallow bays and has been known to eat reindeer!

## Seal hunter

The plentiful supply of seals means a very large, fierce hunter can survive here, too – the polar bear. Ringed seals are the bears' favourite food. A polar bear will sit by a hole in the ice for hours, so that it can pounce on a seal when it pops up to breathe.

## Land of seals and walruses

Walruses and seals are common in the Arctic. They dive into the water to hunt and rest on coastal rock or floating ice shelves.

▼ Walruses aren't very furry, but they have blubber (a thick, fatty layer) under their skin to keep them warm.

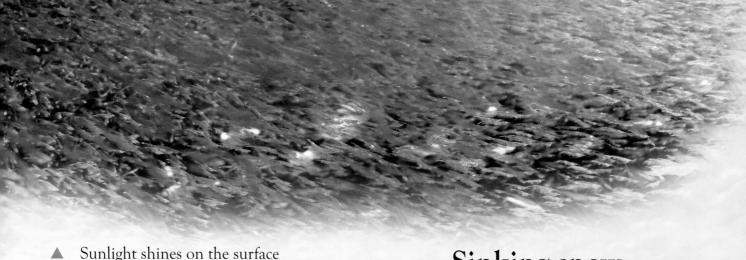

# Deeper down

Deep down in the oceans, below about 500 metres, live some of the strangest, oddest-looking creatures of all. The water at these depths is extremely dark, and it is very cold.

## Sinking snow

Plant plankton needs sunlight to grow. It cannot grow in the deep, dark sea. Deep ocean creatures use another type of food, called 'marine snow', which sinks down from the waters above. It is made up of dead plants and animals, food leftovers and animal poo.

▼ Japanese spider crabs can be almost three metres wide and live at depths of up to 600 metres.

# Sea pigs

Sea pigs live on the deep, dark seabed. They are actually a type of sea cucumber, and are related to starfish. They feed by munching through the muddy ooze on the seabed. It is filled with bits of food from marine snow that has collected there.

▲ Sea pigs are not like real pigs. But you can see how they got their nickname!

## Deep-sea scavengers

Hagfish feed on dead bodies. They release lots of slime to make themselves slippery, so predators can't grab them. They also use their slime to clog up the gills of hunting fish such as sharks.

Sea pens are plant-like animals that stand up from the muddy floor on deep ocean plains. They filter water to catch drifting bits of food.

## The squid and the whale

The giant squid and the sperm whale can be found in the deep sea. This is especially amazing for the sperm whale, as it has to resurface to breathe air. It can hold its breath for 90 minutes to dive as deep as 3,000 metres. It does this to hunt the giant squid.

▲ ▼ Giant squid can be up to 13 metres long. They try to fight off sperm whales by tearing at them with their razor-edged suckers.

# Shining lights

In the pitch-black ocean depths, the only sources of light are the living things themselves. Many deep-sea dwellers have lights on their bodies. Light made by living things is called bioluminescence.

▲ A deep-sea anglerfish, on the prowl for prey in the dark.

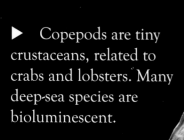

▶ Copepods are tiny crustaceans, related to crabs and lobsters. Many deep-sea species are bioluminescent.

## Lights as lures

The female anglerfish has a light on a stalk above its head, to attract other animals. When they come to take a closer look – SNAP! – the anglerfish gobbles them up.

## I'm over here!

Bioluminescence helps some sea creatures to find each other in the darkness, so that they can mate and have babies. Some hatchetfish are thought to do this, as well as tiny, deep-sea crustaceans called copepods.

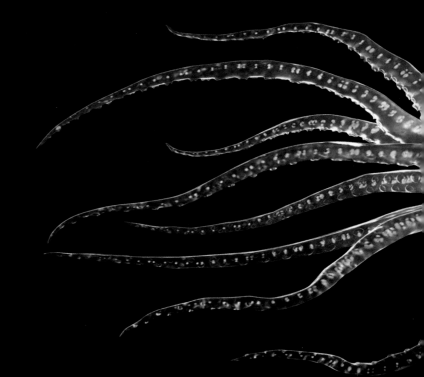

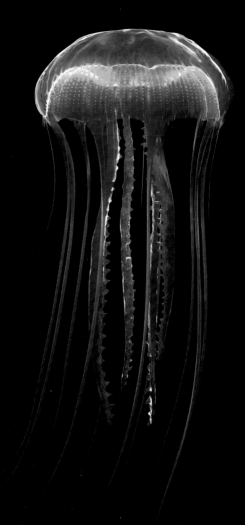

▶ Many jellyfish, like this one, glow with a gentle, blueish light.

## Flashing lights

Flashing lights – suddenly – can be a good way to give a predator a fright, giving smaller fish time to escape. One deep-sea squid uses the same method to confuse and stun its prey, to make it easier to catch.

▼ This pelagic octopus is one of the very few octopuses known to give off light.

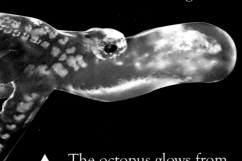

▲ The octopus glows from special suckers, arranged in rows along its arms – like fairy lights.

## Glowing decoys

The vampire squid can squirt glowing, snot-like mucus from its arms. The predator chases this while the squid escapes. A similar decoy (a trick of distraction) is used by the bomber worm. It carries tiny, glowing 'bombs' on its head. When attacked, it drops the bombs and swims away!

▶ Eelpout fish prey upon deep-sea copepods and crabs.

▲ Giant tube worms grow to more than two metres long. Their bodies contain bacteria that feed on minerals in the water. They turn the minerals into food that the worm shares.

# Vents and smokers

The inside of the Earth is made of hot, partly melted rock. In some parts of the seabed, water seeps into cracks and gets heated to boiling point, or even hotter. The hot water then bubbles back out through gaps in the seabed, known as hydrothermal vents.

## Hydrothermal vents

Scientists first discovered the vents in 1977, in water 2,500 metres deep, near the Galapagos Islands in the Pacific Ocean. They were amazed to see not only the hot water jets, but also an amazing variety of living things around them that had never been seen before.

# Black smokers

Some water coming from a vent contains dark-coloured minerals, and looks like black smoke pouring into the sea. These vents are called black smokers. As the cloudy water comes out, bits of the minerals collect around the vents. They build up and up, forming tall chimneys.

▼ In this photo you can see giant tube worms and vent crabs on the far left.

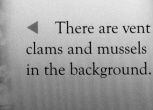

◄ There are vent clams and mussels in the background.

# Eating minerals

Vent creatures do not depend on sunlight for their food. Minerals get dissolved into water as it heats up under the seabed. Bacteria around the vents then convert these minerals into food, which other vent animals can then feed on.

# The Southern Ocean

Around the South Pole of the Earth, there is a large, freezing-cold continent called Antarctica. It is surrounded by the Southern Ocean. The waters here are icy cold, and often freeze over, but they are full of wildlife.

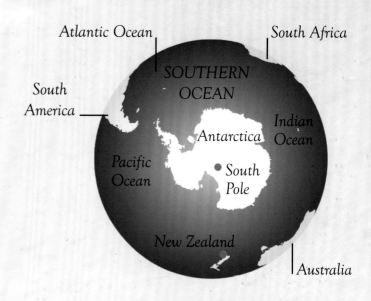

The Southern Ocean lies around Antarctica and is surrounded by the three largest oceans.

## Penguin colonies

Penguins are among the most common animals in Antarctica. The types found here include chinstrap, gentoo, King and Adelie penguins. When they're not diving into the sea for food, they come ashore to mate, lay eggs and care for their chicks.

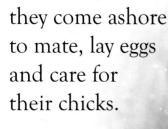

▶ A colony of chinstrap penguins can contain more than a million of them.

Crabeater seals are often found around sea ice, where they can easily go hunting for krill.

## Get your fill of krill

The sea here is bursting with Antarctic krill. They feed on plant plankton, and on ice algae growing on the underside of sea ice. Lots of the animals that live here feed on the krill, such as crabeater seals, blue whales and penguins.

Orcas prefer to eat seals, but will hunt penguins when there are fewer seals around.

## Hungry hunters

Orcas, or killer whales, are common here. They grow up to nine metres long, have very sharp teeth and hunt in groups. They can snatch penguins and seals from the water, or force them off the ice into the sea. Some orcas even surf up onto beaches to grab seals from dry land.

# Oceans in danger

The oceans are big, yet delicate. Sea creatures need the right food and shelter, as well as water that's clean, not too hot and not too cold. Sadly, humans have caused a lot of damage to the sea and its wildlife, and the oceans are also getting warmer.

▼ The scalloped hammerhead shark is endangered due to overfishing.

## Overfishing

Our methods of catching fish and seafood are now so good that we are sometimes in danger of wiping out certain animals. Other creatures, such as dolphins and seabirds, also suffer by getting trapped in fishing nets.

▼ Oil floats on water, so when it leaks from ships it forms a 'slick' on the surface. Marine animals can then get coated in it.

## Pollution

Waste chemicals can flow into rivers and end up in the sea, making seawater dirty or poisonous to sea creatures. Tankers sometimes leak oil into the sea, and the noises they make can confuse animals such as dolphins, which use sounds to communicate and find their way.

◄ Global warming threatens to destroy the habitat of animals such as polar bears.

## NOT SO AWESOME!

In the North Pacific Ocean, the swirling currents have collected millions of bits of plastic rubbish into a huge clump, known as the Great Pacific Garbage Patch. The plastic can make sea creatures ill if they accidentally swallow it.

# Warmer waters

When certain waste gases are released into the atmosphere, they trap heat from the sun. This causes global temperatures to rise. As seas warm up, polar ice melts. This is bad news for sea creatures such as krill, polar bears and penguins, as they need sea ice to hunt, feed or breed on.

▼ Dolphins navigate and find food using 'echolocation'. They do this by making sounds and collecting the echoes as they bounce off objects.

# What can we do?

People should never leave litter on beaches or drop it off boats. Many countries have now made it illegal to dump chemical waste into the sea, and are trying to encourage people to use less fuel and energy so that we can slow down the process of global warming. New laws help to prevent overfishing and protect endangered species.

# Glossary

**Adapted** Gradually developed to suit a particular purpose.

**Algae** Tiny, plant-like living things.

**Bacteria** A type of very small, very simple living thing (made up of just one cell).

**Bioluminescence** Light naturally created and given off by some types of living things.

**Cartilage** A bendy, rubbery substance found in the skeleton of some animals.

**Coral** A hard, shell-like substance made by coral polyps.

**Coral polyps** Tiny sea creatures, related to jellyfish, that live together in groups.

**Coral reef** A large coral structure built up by many generations of coral polyps.

**Current** A fast-flowing stream of water within an ocean, sea, river or lake.

**Decay** To rot or break down.

**Digest** To take in food and break it down into useful substances for a living thing.

**Diurnal** Active during the day.

**Ecosystem** A community of living things that interact with each other and their habitat.

**Endangered** In danger of dying out.

**Equator** The invisible 'central line' that runs around the middle of the planet.

**Fresh water** Water that is not in the seas and oceans – and is not salty – such as river water.

**Gills** Body parts used to take in oxygen from water, enabling the animal to breathe.

**Habitat** The surroundings where a living thing is found and is suited to surviving in.

**Hemisphere** One half of the Earth.

**Ice shelf** A thick, permanent layer of ice attached to the land but floating on the sea.

**Krill** Very small, shrimp-like sea creatures that swim in huge shoals or swarms.

**Marine** Describes things to do with the seas and oceans.

**Migrate** To travel long distances, to find food or to mate and have babies.

**Mucus** A slimy, snotty substance produced by many living things.

**Mudflats** Large, flat areas of seashore made up of mud or muddy sand.

**Nerves** Fibres in the body that sense things and carry signals around the body.

**Nocturnal** Active during the night.

**Nutritious** Containing a lot of useful food.

**Organism** Another name for a living thing.

**Oxygen** A gas that animals need to breathe, which is found in both air and water.

**Pelagic zone** The open part of the ocean, away from the coast.

**Plankton** Tiny plants and animals that drift around in seawater.

**Predator** An animal that hunts and feeds on other animals.

**Prehistoric** From the time before humans began writing and recording things.

**Prey** An animal that is hunted and eaten by another animal.

**Reef** Any structure or object in the ocean, close to the sea surface.

**Scavenge** To feed on old, dead animals, or bits of food left by other animals.

**School (or shoal)** A large group of fish swimming together.

**Sediment** Material such as sand, mud or slime that settles on seabeds and riverbeds.

**Species** Living things of the same species, or type, can mate and produce offspring (babies).

**Streamlined** Smooth and pointed in shape, for moving quickly through water or air.

**Tropical** Belonging to the hottest parts of the Earth, on both sides of the equator.

**Venom** A poisonous substance that an animal injects into its enemies or prey.

**Wildlife reserve** An area that is kept safe and protected to give wildlife a place to live.

**Zooplankton** Tiny animal plankton.

# Index

# Further Information

## BOOKS

**Research on the Edge: Oceans**
By Angela Royston (Wayland, 2014)

**Weird Sea Creatures**
By Erich Hoyt (Firefly Books, 2013)

**First Animal Encyclopedia**
By Anita Ganeri (A & C Black, 2013)

**Discover More: Ocean and Sea**
By Steve Parker (Scholastic, 2012)

## ONLINE RESOURCES

**The National Oceans and Atmospheric Administration (USA)**
Lots to explore on the NOAA's kids pages: http://oceanservice.noaa.gov/kids/

**Natural History Museum, London, UK**
Visit the Life in the Sea pages: http://www.nhm.ac.uk/kids-only/life/life-sea/